TO A GIRL
I HAVEN'T MET

To A Girl
I Haven't Met

zack grey

ISBN: 978-0-692-94700-5

Contents:

Forgive me,
I sometimes don't believe in you.
I hope you won't
hold this against me,
but rather find it endearing
because I must
continually
find my faith.

I don't know when we'll meet or if this will ever see the light of day but I want you to know right now that I can't stop thinking about you. In my mind your voice is clear. Sharp, but soft. You, like me, are a very contradictory person. You are a bumblebee that should not be able to fly, but you do. You carry your heavy burdens and your past everywhere you go and they look beautiful on you as you soar.

I've written this book as a testament to my faith. That you exist. That the universe will bring us together. That I'll know you when I see you. I want to know everything about you — but first, it's only fair that you know everything about me.

To People I've Loved Before

I have a poet's heart; I fall fast and hard like a stone dropped from a ten story building. Naturally, I have loved many people before and I have been broken many times before— don't be sad for me— it's beautiful and I'd want to be no different. But I want you to know about them. I want you to know about the ways I've loved and the ways I've been hurt because this journey is what has made me the person you will love. The person that will love you with every last breath. These are words I have written to the people that I loved before.

16

16

The First

We were notes
left in lockers
and i's dotted with hearts,
friends used as carrier
pigeons
and favorite songs on the
radio.

In the end,
really,
we were just two
kids in love.

We were young then,
but I'll never forget that
you loved me when I
didn't even love myself.

We have become
so scarred
by this world that
doesn't accept us
dreamers, lovers
& thinkers,
that the
wonder of
young love
is impossible
for us now.

I wish we could
remove this
sallow adult
skin
and love
like children
again.

I said I loved you and I meant it then.
Why do we have to judge things
based on how they end?

All I wanted was you,
but you didn't want me,
you wanted a
                fantasy.

In the end,
love wasn't what
tore us
apa rt;

It was a
sep a ra tion
of bodies
that made us feel
separated
at the
soul.

I believed in us
& you just
believed in me.

I think you must've forgot.

That your own family had turned their backs on you and treated you like you were nothing, but I? I was right there. I barely knew you— in fact we'd only met once. I thought you would have forgotten me. Or at least that you would pretend you had like most girls do. But you didn't— we had made a mark on each other after just one meeting and we both laughed about our silly teenager haircuts and how we were both awkward at first conversations.

It was sparks. You didn't know anyone else who appreciated intelligent conversation so much and neither did I and sometimes you were sad too, and I was there for that. I was there for everything until you pushed me away.

And let me remind you of the third time we found ourselves close again: years had passed after you made it clear that you weren't interested in being friends (even though I'd never treated you like anything less than absolutely lovable just the way you already were) but I ignored the fact that you were the one that cut me off and not the other way around. By then I'd decided to live my life in a simple way. I was telling everyone the positive things I thought about them, even if they had hurt me before (I still do).

I texted to remind you how pleasant it used to be to quote song lyrics to each other and know that the other person could be absolutely relied on to know the rest. And even then you barely tolerated me (you treated me like the kid brother you put up with just because mom told you to, but everyone knows the kid brother always cramps your vibe).

I think the hardest part is that after all this, I saw you the other day and I still smiled in your direction. I would've even played nice and pretended you had never left any bruises on my heart, but you turned away.
You wouldn't. Even. Look. At. Me.

I sit here now and rack my brain as to why you've made such an effort to separate yourself from me. What did I do wrong?
I think I finally have an answer:

Apparently,
the only thing I
did wrong was

care about you.

18

The Unrequited

You've taught me
to be great at
pretending.
Every day I'm pretending
like I don't want to
call you beautiful
and tell you that
I see the whole
universe
in your eyes.
I pretend that
I'm okay with
calling you friend
but the truth is it
burns because
when I think about you
(which is all the time)
there's a fire
in my chest.
And just for my own
sanity, I pretend
that no matter how this
turns out
I'll be okay.
I pretend.

I need to take some
time off from you,
even though I am
always wishing for
your heart
to be beating
right next to mine.
I want you to miss
me the way that I
miss you
all the time.

It's a shame that you're
kept up late into the night
with thoughts of someone
that had your heart and
refused to take care of it.
And I know, I tend to speak
when I should be silent and
give advice when the comfort
of human presence is
all that's needed, but I just
want to remind you of one more
thing before I sit in silence and
dream the beat of our hearts into
synchronizing. There are only two
types of people in this world:
those who break hearts and

those who have them.

zack grey

You were
bleeding
for him
while I was
bleeding
for you.

You built the
Great Wall of China
in your heart
to keep out the
invaders.

I asked you
one day
how I could
prove that I'm
the one worth
letting in
and you said
you didn't
know.

Let me ask you,
are you familiar
with ancient
history?

Even the real thing
only took eight
years to break
through.

You don't know
how patient I am
do you?

I'm so lost in
loving you
I'm not sure
if it's you
that I love
or the idea
of what you
might be.

With you,
I always feel
like I'm losing
something
I never had.

It hurts me that I
can't help you,
that I can't take
the pain away or
stitch your wounds
or simply kiss your
forehead and make
you feel safe. It
hurts that you hurt
and I wish that just
saying that aloud
was enough to
change everything.

I
love
you.
There,
I said it.
And now it's
time for me to
admit something
else: I have to let you
go, because I finally see
that you will never love me
as much as
I
love
you.

20

The One That Vanished

I saved your letters
and put them away in
a box, labeled
"pretty,
useless things".

I still wear the bracelet
you bought me in Rome.
The clasp is weak and
if I don't pay attention it
comes undone and falls away;

I remember that's how
you lost the one
I bought you before we
ever got home.

I should have known then and
taken it as the sign it was:
that everything we had was fleeting. Momentary.
That tomorrow you would be
gone and you'd never think of
me again, but I, all these years
later, would be left
with nothing but
tiny pieces of you.

I needed you,
but you
just needed me
to need you.

We had a tradition for letting
each other know the
importance of what we
were about to say. I
don't know who started it—
me or you— but we'd
talk in the silliest cockney
accents you could imagine
and say whatever we were
thinking. That was our way
of making the pain feel just
a little bit less. Together.
Now you're gone and I still talk
in a funny accent sometimes
but it doesn't help how it used to.
Now I'm just talking to myself
and it's always about you.

You taught me that
it's possible for
someone to leave
while they're still
sitting
right by your side.

We used to talk about how
much it hurts when
people leave,
and I told you it didn't even
hurt me anymore
because I always
expected it.
Just like all the others,
you told me you were
different.
"I'll be the one who
stays,"
you said.
Now you're gone and
I'm wondering—
are you a hypocrite
for leaving,
or am I
for believing you
when you said you wouldn't?

You left and you
left yourself
behind.

Your lingering scent,
the way you'd laugh
when I messed up the
lyrics to our favorite songs,
the feeling of your fingers
resting softly against my
spine.

I tried packing it all into suitcases
and tossing them into the river of
yesterday's long passed,
but no matter how many times
I throw away these leftover
pieces of you
they all come back.

And now I'll never be able
to love with open hands again
because they will always be
carrying this baggage
you left me with.

I always thought you'd
come back to me,
if only briefly.
I've never been
able to understand
how someone
could
get rid of a part of themselves
so easily.

Would you come back
just long enough
to teach me?

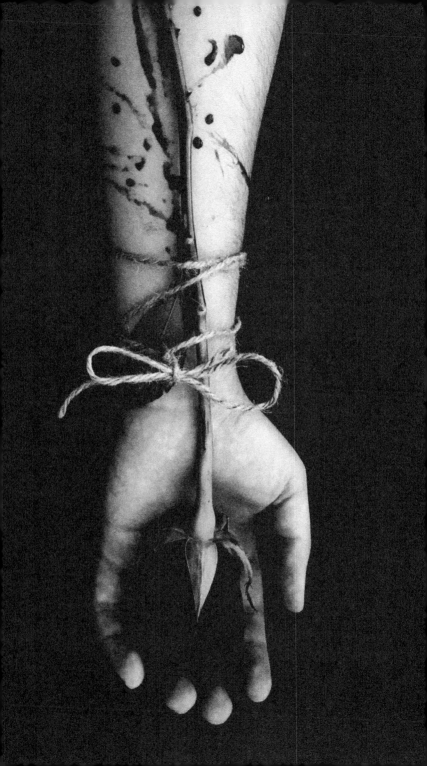

21

The One That Broke Me

I remember the last time I saw you. It was a Wednesday night in a public place, surrounded by mutual 'friends'. People you thought of as friends and people I put up with just to breathe the same air as you.

You were wearing a loose floral print dress and there was a sterling silver heart dangling from your neck. You were showing off the man who just asked you to marry him— you said yes of course and internally I said no but what was I to do? Make a scene? I should've been clearer but I wasn't and that's my fault.

And now you were in love. So was I, but who am I to try to take your smile away from him? Away from you? Just to find my own amidst the broken pieces of the two of you.
Nothing good starts that way, I knew.

I sat in a corner with a cold drink in hand, trying my best to pretend I wasn't watching you. Trying my best to pretend I wasn't sick to the stomach with love and jealousy. Trying my best to pretend that I was just fine. (Truth: I. Was. Not.)
The way he smiled at you was so soft, it softened you even. An exuberant character if I knew one, suddenly calm and waiting for someone to lead her.

You walked by one time and took that single opportunity to destroy my soul with hope: "If not for him, it would be you."
That's what you said to me, and I died for so many reasons.

It's been 3 years. Now I'm more than old enough to ask for an alcoholic beverage in a public place and not be thrown out. I still think of you. I guess that's apparent. Or it would be if you ever saw this.

I checked my phone the other day to see what pieces of you remained. That cute voicemail you sent me when you were dizzy after having your blood drawn is gone from my saved messages and the gift I gave you before you left is gone now.(Your mom gave it back to me when you took off with him. I was mad and hurt: sold it. Cried.)

Every trace of what you used to be is wiped from the internet and I don't even have a single photo of you left. Oh, and the tiny notes you wrote when you visited me in between days with him? I burned those and rubbed the ashes on my face. (They say ash is a great exfoliator.)

Now I'm just left with memories that I have to carry on my own, because you refuse to share them with me and I can't get rid of them.
Yeah, I remember all right.

It's a shame
that you hated
everything I loved,
because one of
those things
was you.

I don't want to stop
feeling this pain because
if I do, I'll have to face the
truth: that it wasn't love
after all.

In my memory we sat at a cafe table. I was too nervous to need caffeine, but I bought a drink while I waited for you just to occupy my hands. I picked a table outside so no one would hear all of the embarrassing things I was about to say, and as I sat my legs shook uncontrollably. By the time you arrived— waltzing across the parking lot, dodging cars and people effortlessly like a trained dancer— there were rings of condensation on the table and my hands were cold even though it was hot outside.

You were wearing a sundress made of cotton and big sunglasses like it was just another day of your breezy life.
I was sweating and you were waiting for some kind of big revelation.

"I-," I began, choking from the start, unable to get over myself. "I had so much to say until I saw you, but now the words are gone."

"It's okay," you said, "take your time."

And as many times as I replay this moment in my head, I can't remember any of the words that I finally said. I just remember that at the end, I told you that how you felt about him was how I felt about you.

"That sounds miserable," you said.

"It is," I replied.

And then you left.

And I was still sitting there and water rings were still on the table, but it was like you'd never arrived. You left as perfectly— as cleanly— as you had entered.

If only you could've left my head the same way.

You said
"goodbye"
like it was
just a word
and it wouldn't
take my breath away.

When I was in love,
I wondered. If the heart
grows heavy both ways
how is falling in love any
different than falling out of it?
And when you wouldn't let me
love you anymore, I learned.
The difference is want.
When I loved you I wanted
to be sick.
And when you were gone
I just wanted someone to
take the pain away.

When you go
you take my
stories with you,
that I cannot change.
But today I begin a new
story: one that
you're not in.

And if I ever see you again,
my only wish is for you
to know how far I've
gone without you.

23

The One That Healed Me

I once said that you
were an invader
of hearts because
you got to me at
a time when I just
wanted to heal on
my own, and now
I think—
if only invaders
throughout history
had tried to understand
each other the way that
you tried to
understand me, then
maybe, just maybe,
history wouldn't be
quite so
dreary.

And even
as our love
is growing
I can feel it
fading
a
w
a
y
.

You told me you were
in a bathtub crying
when you called,
just like in
all the movies.

And I simply wished we
could have our airport
reunion scene, just
like in all the movies.

I tell myself everyday
that it's better than
being numb.
I wish I knew a way to
live that doesn't involve
always hurting.
Did you even know
that your hurt was
hurting me too?

The last time
we
    said
"I love you",
    I cried
more than
you did.

I'm happy that you
hurt me;

for the first time
in years,
I can
        feel.

Something.

Anything.

I
can
feel.

You were not
my destination
but I thank you
for being a much
needed rest stop
along the way.

We will never love
someone else
quite the same way
that we loved each other;
& in that,
there is something both
sad & beautiful.

If we tattooed the hurt on our arms
and slow danced together,
maybe the lacing of our fingers,
the rhythmic drawl of our bodies
moving in unison,
the feeling of finally working for something
together,
even if it's just dancing
long enough to make it through one
overly-covered 80's song,

maybe that's all it would take to
silence the killing whispers of,
"I dont think you understand me".

I still hope
        and I
still dream
that even if it's
not you,
you will draw her out.
You will whisper in her ear.
You will tell her that I
am so far from perfect,
but she will learn
to love my
imperfections
just as you did.

I still hope and I still
dream that you
will be a
catalyst
for so much more.

I hope and I dream
and I wish and I wonder
and I imagine and believe
that she's still out there
looking for me.

What Makes Me Different

I wish that I were easy to open, like a book with well-thumbed pages, soft cracks in the spine, dogeared at the corners. But I am a closed journal, locked and keyless. I write these words to you because I know that I may never be able to speak them aloud. I am nothing like anyone you've ever met before, or ever will meet again. I want you to see how. I want you to know what makes me different than all the others that came before me and why you can be certain I'll love you better than they did.

Allow me to tell you about
my flaws:
sometimes I'm too loud
and more often I'm too quiet.
I don't know how to comfort
those who are crying
or grieve those who've died,
and I have opinions on things
that I have no right to.
Sometimes I'm nice to those
who don't deserve it
and often I'm not
to those who do.
I love fiercely,
but I don't show it
as well as I'd like.
And the truth is that
the list is never-ending
because I'm a mess.
A disaster.
Human.

I don't know if I can
love you
if your heart
isn't broken
in the same places as mine.

I've scraped knees
and twisted ankles,
been bit by dogs
and cut my fingers,
but nothing hurts
as much as a
broken heart.

I always hear how little girls
are raised with unrealistic
fairytale expectations of love
and knights in shining armor,
but so was I— all the stories
taught me to believe that
It just takes courage and
confidence to save anyone.
What they all fail to mention
is that sometimes the dragon
is within her,
and try as you might, it's not possible
to save someone from a beast
that even they don't see.

Did you know I'm
riddled with holes?
Not enough to kill me,
just enough to let the
light shine through.

The truth is,
my soul never was
happy in that
tiny little
box.

Some days
I wake up
and wonder
when I will be
comfortable
in this
new skin.

Sometimes I hurt
the one I love
by loving them
entirely
before they are
entirely ready
to be loved.

zack grey

I look out
through
glass eyes
at glass people
in glass houses
and see nothing
but glass lives
so easily
broken.

I can't hold a conversation
without looking away;
the eyes carry a weight
too intense
for me to bear.

Be my reason to
focus.
Take away the
pain of my
empathy.

When a room is full,
so am I.
I can feel every beat
of every heart,
and every nervous thought.
I can feel the sweat on
a person's palms without
shaking their hand
and I

am overwhelmed.

And while I've been taught
to show love toward all,
it was only through my own
experience that I learned
some people can only be
loved from afar.

I sit at the cafe and I observe her working.
Her hair is tied up in a loose bun and she's got
trendy reading glasses on as she sits alone at a
table for four. Spread out in front of her, there's
a Mac computer, textbooks, and papers that
look like they could use some shuffling.

I'm trying to focus on work of my own, but
sometimes out of the corner of my eye I see her
bite her pen and her left foot is tucked under
her right leg, while her other foot is tapping
softly on the floor.

I'm wondering what she's studying so hard
for. If she's always bit her pen and shook with
nerves and curled up into herself. If she's as
scared of home as I am because she doesn't
know what "home" really is.

She looks up from her work and catches me
looking before I can avert my eyes. In that
instant I see it. She's made her home in other
people too. People that didn't want to share it
with her. People that had their own homes and
didn't invite her in. People that saw her with
her hair down and didn't appreciate how rare a
sight that is.

I wish I could walk up and tell her that home
is herself. That they didn't love themselves
and that's why they could never love her. That
really, no matter how hard it is to believe, the
truth is that there's nothing wrong with her.
That she's perfectly imperfect just the way she
is.

I don't walk over to her and I don't say any of
these things,
because I'm just
projecting.

My back has
been rebelling
against me
since I was
a teenager,
but only
now have I
begun to
wonder
if it was
already
tired of
holding up
the weight
of the world.

zack grey

I take all of my vitamins
with wine
to mend the
broken parts
and calm
my restless mind.

I am not James Dean, but I did die young.
I died as a cynic and was reborn
in the fire of tenderness,
peace and resilient love.
I've never lived a life of excess
but I know the drive of always wanting
more, more, more,
and in that I've died too.
I am not a movie star
and I am not a master thief of hearts,
but I do demand that you look into

my eyes
and drown in my soul.
I want more than anything
just to be
seen,
to be grasped and understood
and accepted.
Not by the whole world,
just by mine.
Just by you.
And if I must
die young
again
to find you,
I will.

If I could talk to him,
the boy that became the man,
I'd tell him that he was
doing it right all along.
It's okay to be different.
It's okay that they don't
understand you,
they were not meant to.
Love yourself and just know
your tribe will find you soon.

I didn't used to appreciate the sea as a man
should.
Narrow-minded, I focused on how she swells and
violently tosses anyone who dares to enter. That
was before I visited her at night. Before I saw how
beautiful she is in darkness, only illuminated by
the soft glow of moonlight reflecting from every
ripple. That was before I felt the chill of her air
making my hair stand on end.
And now when I am before her, foam lapping
at my toes, the smell of salt tickling my nose,
I imagine the waves smoothing my hair as she
sings to me, "Child, it's not over yet".

Warning:
I like spicy food
and music that
bares the rawness
of the soul.
I like my drinks
extra strong
and I love people
who hold on just
a little bit
too tight.

I guess what I'm
trying to tell you
is that I'm an intense
person and if you
can't handle that
you can just stay
safely tucked away
in your
subtle world
and watch me
as I continue to
devour my own.

My head
understands
things that
my heart
is not
willing
to accept.

As much as I love words
they plague me every night
like someone I have wronged.
They swirl above my bed
and infiltrate my head,
whispering, "speak us,
tell them all that we
are here."
And so I do, because
despite the awful
inconvenience to me,
I know they do
spiteful things
just to find their way
to you.
So that you can laugh.
So that you can smile.
So that you can love.
And so,
that maybe,
you can heal.

I have hit road
                bumps.
I have been wrong and
been wrong and been wrong
and I swear I will be wrong
a thousand times more,
but I am willing to be wrong
as many times as it takes to
finally be right,
                when it comes
                to you.

Honestly I don't
even try to be
clever like the
rest of them;
I know I can
never measure up.
I just want you to
see my words and
understand that
you're the
inspiration for
every single one.

If only you
could see
the way I smile
in my sleep,
just knowing that
you exist.

I believe
in all things
imaginary,
because the
world I live in
is imaginary too,
and more than
anything I believe in
imaginary you.

I find sadness beautiful,
and I just know you'll have
sad eyes.

I can't wait to make them
glimmer with
hope.

I'm only alone
when I lose
myself.

When someone engages me in conversation, I often can't look them in the eyes. I can't focus on what they're saying or how their lips are moving and my attenion is darting around the room, settling on the slightest turn of a doorknob or the landing of a butterfly or the sound pieces of cloth make when they rub together.

I know this is not normal and I wish I could find my center in the person sitting in front of me but I only ever feel like wherever I am and whoever I'm talking to it's not the right person. My fears are not calmed. My confidence is not gained. I am a skeptic and and and
anxious and I don't want anyone to see so I do these things
to avoid letting anyone look behind my eyes and find the truth
in the space between.

I have never said any of these things in so much detail before and I'm only doing it now so you understand when I find you. So you can see in that moment that I'm not saying things just to flatter your perfect ears. So that, when I look in your eyes and find myself at home, you'll believe me when I say I never want to leave.

My placid face
betrays little
emotion,
but I feel
everything.

A crescent moon scars my thumb
and a slash on my index finger
keeps it company.
Puncture marks pepper my
right foot, feeling a little
lonely.
My skin sings,
"here's a mark,
there's a mark,"
and I can't help but to think,
if only,
if only the good moments
would mark my body
the way pain does.

I wish I could know
what I was missing,

but I've been so deeply
bred with indifference toward

anyone who's different despite
the fact that I'm different

from anyone
I've ever known,

it's hard to miss
what I never knew.

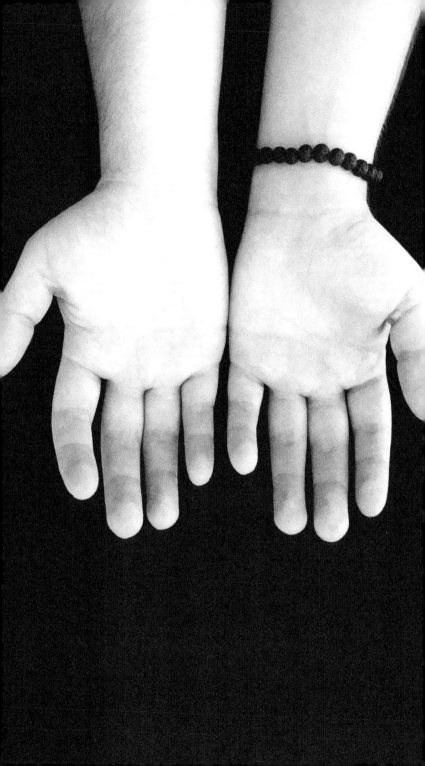

All I have are
these hands.
They are not
very strong or
calloused,
nor are they particularly
nimble or skilled.

All I have are
these hands
to channel my
spirit
into this pen
and write these words.

All I have are
these hands to
carry all of the
love that I
give you.

All I have are these
hands to
bring you
close.
Will you
hold them?

I like books
more than people
and rain
more than shine
because I am
nothing like
the rest of them
on the inside.

I am a different
kind of different
and I just want to
find a girl who's
different enough
to be perfectly
normal with me.

I always leave
parties
early,

but I never leave
a good conversation
before I
have to.

zack grey

The only thing I do
constantly is change,
but I can promise that
the only thing that will
never change is
me loving you.

While I Wait:
thoughts & dreams

While I wait for you, I am still looking
in my mind. Passively searching. Hoping
beyond hope that I can simply dream our
meeting into existence. I daydream about you,
I nightdream about you, I think about you
all the time. What you look like, if you like
to dance or if you're a wallflower like me,
how you take your coffee, or maybe you
don't like coffee at all, preferring tea instead.
These things matter not at all and more
than anything in the world simultaneously.

Dive into my mind. I want you to know exactly
what I've been thinking and
dreaming about all this time.

You could say that I'm tired.
Tired of looking, tired of waiting—
but I understand that this is the
process. It's how I refine myself
for you. And when the time comes,
I will be a shot of whiskey, distilled
three times over, just strong enough
to get you drunk on my love.

There is a place for you in my dreams,
right between Paris and Barcelona.
You are the adventure I seek,
the journey I want to take
and hope never ends.

I've dreamt
about you for an
embarrassingly long time.

I've imagined the way
you laugh so many different
ways they've all blended
together now into one
sound that I swear is perfect.

I already love you and
I've never even
seen your face.

For you
I am always waiting,
and for you
I don't mind.

I show these things to the world,
but only so you can see
that my world is you,
and one day I will be yours,
hopefully.

Sometimes,
the tears on
my pillow
grow legs.
They find their
way to you
and keep you
company
through the night.
And when you
wake from this
Nightmare,
you'll see that
you were never alone.

I have loved many people
that never loved me back.
I have left parts of me in
other hearts that can
never be extracted,
parts that can never be returned
or found in other places.
Once a piece of me is
gone I know it's never
coming back, but I
have one chance to be
saved:
              if you, by some
miracle of the universe
are left with the remainder
of jigsaw pieces in your
heart that are missing from
my own,
god, we'll make the
most beautiful
p
  u
z
    z
l
      e
you've ever seen.

There will be things about you
that are difficult to take.
You and I will have strong
opposing opinions and
neither of us will admit
we're wrong because we've
both been at this so long.
We've both grown accustomed
to ourselves and comfortable
with our old ways. We will often
argue about pointless things,
but the whole time I will smile.
I won't be able to think about
anything but how cute you are
when you're angry and that will
make you angrier. And I will
laugh, and you will remember that's
why you fell for me in the first
place— I can never stay mad at you.

I've been looking for you in the
                        cre vic es,
the cra/cks
            in the walls-

                in the space between

this moment and the one in which
I find you.

            I look,
                    knowing that eyes
are not strong enough to find something
so easy to miss. You won't be obvious—
you'll be an enigma I work to
                            u
                              n
                            r
                        a
                          v
                            e
                        l

and only when I do will I find that you were
always
seep
    ing
       through.

I just have to slip off these uncomfortable
thoughts,
put on something cozy

          (close my eyes)

and concentrate to see
that I am always

       b r e a t h i n g i n

        your essence.

On many late nights
I can't sleep because I'm
missing you.

I get up and
tip-toe
to my window,
look out and
gaze into the
veil of night.

That's how I
remind myself
that we're under
the same sky,
and somehow,
that is enough.

As I sit here I realize
that someone else
has been on a plane
with you before, that
someone else has looked
across the aisle and observed
you with your legs crossed, hair
falling in your face as you
lean in to your work
and someone else
has seen you quietly
rule the world from a
window seat.

It's exhausting,
always
missing you.

I don't know why I keep
wondering. I've known
for quite some time now
how we'll meet. One day
my book will be published,
and when it's accepted
more than it has any right
to be, I will be sent to sit
at tables and squiggle lines
on blank pages for days
on end. I will be forced to
patiently wade through crowds,
shake hands and say "no, thank
you!" to every person I meet.
But all of this will be worth it,
because just when my head is
buried in a book, attempting
to sign it in a way that makes
my handwriting seem better than
it is, you will be right in front of me.
You will hand my words to me
and say, "I think these are yours,
I came to give them back to you.
Can we meet for coffee later?"

How can I miss you
when I
haven't even met you?

In my dreams you're sipping
coffee with Sylvia Plath
resting comfortably in your
lap. When I wake, there's a
faint memory of green which
explains why I can't
pass a Starbucks without entering.
One of these times you will
be there. And when I enter,
the right side of your mouth
will curl up in a half smile, and
you'll say, "I took the liberty of
ordering for you. I hope you don't
mind."

And if you're waiting in some invisible plane of
existence, please,
reach your hand out and reel me in.
Save me.
From myself.
From fear of failure.
From all of those that
say I'm right to be afraid.
Come closer and take me
away from here. Take me to where you are
so I can get lost in another
dimension.
So I can get lost in
                   you.

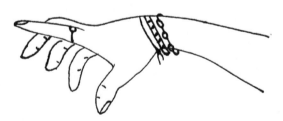

I think about you all the time.
To me,
that
is

poetry.

I have left a
       path
            for
                you
          to
       follow.

I have left fragments of my heart
and words that I had to brave violent
oceans to find.

I have left dreams behind,
patiently waiting for you to
return them to me.

And just in case none of that works,
I leave a trail of blood
dripping with each movement I make.

Cut me open and remind me
that love
         still bleeds red.
Please,

find your way to me.

There's a place in my mind
where I just sit and think of you.
You see, it's not that I can't live
without you. I love the peace of this
emptiness just like I love a tree that
has no leaves. But I do believe that if
this place had a name outside the hazy
dream space of my head, it
would be Loneliness and even if
it takes an eternity, I will
wait for you there,
until you take your spot beside me
and we rename it
together.

I imagine waking up to an empty bed in the morning and worrying that you're gone. As it goes, I will have worried for nothing. I'll walk through the house and find you where you always are first thing in the morning: sitting in the nook right under the window with your legs drawn close to your chest. You're still in your pajamas and wearing no makeup, which is how you look best because your face is already perfect without it.

You have a mug of freshly brewed coffee in one hand and one of your favorite books in the other. You prefer to read the same old novels over and over, because there's nothing like the classics.

You look up from whatever you're reading as I approach and my face is overtaken by a smile because I'm helpless when it comes to your radiant warmth.

This moment will forever be my happy thought.

Even when you're gone, I will think back to you curled up by the window to calm my fears, because there is no fear in you and your courage is contagious. I'll do this over and over. I'll go back and back and back again because that moment will be my first taste of paradise.

And I don't know, maybe paradise only comes once in this lifetime. Maybe paradise is a place for some people and maybe it's a thing or a person for others, but for me

paradise is you.

Maybe my eyes
don't want to shut
because they're afraid
I'll miss you.

I look for your name:
in coffee shops and
at grocery stores
and in the books I
read. I am convinced
that somewhere I will
find pieces of you,
pieces you've shed to
make way for the new
skin you're growing.
And while I search,
every so often I stop
in front of my mirror
and write names in the
dust. Eventually, one of
these names will fit. Maybe
the very act of sliding my
finger through the particles
is enough to call you to me.
Maybe I will turn around and
you will be there. Maybe.

I wonder where
your molecules
have been

and
if parts of you
have danced
on the edge of
the universe.

I wonder if,
when you smile,
will I find stars
between your
teeth?

And
all of the
people you've
met until now,

were they just
preparing you
for me?

I write day and night
sick and insane, lost
and found in the same
moment, in pain but
feeling more alive
than I ever have before,
and it's all about you.

You are my muse.

I hope you will understand
that this is the highest
form of love that I
can give to anyone,
and I choose to
give it all to you.

When I meet you
I'll show you the book
I wrote for you.

"Ah, so you're a poet,"
you'll conclude,
intrigued.

"No, I'm a
storm chaser,"
I'll say.

You'll look at me
with a coy grin,
"How do you figure?"

And I'll smile back,
ever content to play
this game of cat and mouse.

"Well," I'll tell you,
"I have never
fallen in love
with people,
only with
thunderstorms
in human bodies."

I can't bring myself
to take care of these
mundane tasks. The
laundry and the recycling
and the bills I have to pay;
it's amazing the things
I will put off just to
spend another second
thinking of you.

And now I'm
just waiting for
the day when
I can take you
with both hands,
look you deep
an the eye
and with an
adoring sigh
I'll say, "this—
this is the face of
the woman I love."

I often think of the day we'll
meet and the things I'll say
to you. I'll tell you that I've
been missing you my whole
life, and I'll tell you that I never
understood why a girl like you
would give even a moment of
her time to a guy like me, and
you'll laugh as if I must be joking
because there's something you
see in me that I never could.
I'll tell you this cheesy thing
I've been thinking of since the
moment we met and I know
you'll laugh, because how
could you not? But I will
mean it. I will mean every
last word of it when I say
that you're not just one in
a million, you're impossible,
and I'm the world's biggest
fan of
        impossible things.

Maybe we don't have to
find each other first;
it could be second,
third, fourth, fifth,
just end up in my
arms, and until then
I don't care who you're
with.

When We Meet

I won't put you on a pedestal— that's not fair. I won't crush you with the weight of my expectations or ask you for anything more than this: make me want to be better, and I promise I will do everything in my power to make you feel the same way. This is what I imagine it will be like when we meet, the sweet things we'll say to each other, and the ways we'll both grow as we work together to find our place in this universe.

When we
    lock eyes
your world
    will crumble
to the ground,
but don't you
worry, dear,
we can
       build
a new one
together.

I am not a mathematician,
but if I were, I'd find a way
to calculate the square root
of your love, because I
can't seem to shake the
thought that if I just find
the root of everything that
made you love all of the
people before me, maybe
I can make you love me too.

Step into my rhythm,

circadian;

I'll take it slow
just for you,

sliding my palms
softly onto yours...

I'll allow you
to settle in,

and as you
look inside yourself
for trust,

allow me
to show you

it's possible
to walk tenderly
into your life
and have no
intention of

leaving.

I wish I could have you whole,
but I'll take you broken.
And if you let me,
I'll pull you closer
and hold you tight
until the gold flows
and fills the cracks
in your
tired bones.

I don't need you to complete me,
I am whole—
but dear you shine
and I think your light
and my dark
could make a lovely
lunar eclipse

of the soul.

If you
let me in,
you won't
ever need
walls
again.

Maybe it never
worked because
he loved you in the
wrong direction.
He started with
all the right words
and a faux sparkle
in his eyes and
he couldn't or he
wouldn't measure up
to how he started.

.em htiw evol ni llaF

Maybe if I say it
in reverse I can
make you believe
that this time it
won't end the same.

.em htiw evol ni llaF

You don't have to trust
me from the start,
I'd rather work
for your heart
until you see that
it only gets better
and maybe the wrong
direction will become
the right one and
finally,
you will

fall in love with me.

You're the only one
who can take me to heaven
and bring me back to earth
in the same
sentence.

You need
understanding,
not
questioning
eyes.

It's true what they say,
that most men have a one
track mind. But I am
not most men.
I can only focus on
the beautiful look of
destruction
in your eyes.

I must have written
you into existence.
you are the kind of
perfect found only
in fiction.

zack grey

I
see
your
soul
in
your
smile.

The moon
controls
the tides
of the ocean.

You
control
the tides
of my heart.

We have met
before.
Long before the world
that we live in now
came to be,
long before the
sun started revolving
around you,

the stardust that
you are made of

and the stardust that
became me

found each other
and made a promise
that's taken
14 billion years
to keep:

"We will be
 together
 again
 one day."

You are
absolutely,
perfectly,
m   s   e   up.
  e   s   d

Here I am
drowning
in an
ocean
of you.

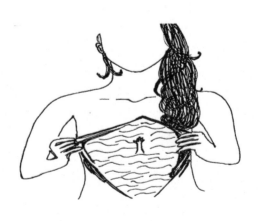

My love for you
is just like the universe:
forever expanding.

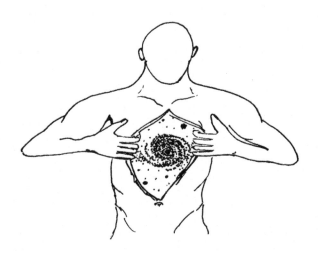

Existence
between worlds:
yours and mine.
It's all I've ever
wanted.

You're a
tortured
soul with
the face
of an
angel.

You heal me
in ways that
I can't
heal myself.

I want to move you.
I want to cross the bridge
between exchanging pleasantries
and seeping down deep into your soul.

I want to say hello
and make you shake
because you know a simple
greeting from me is laced with more
layers than even an 'I love you' from anyone
else.

I want to speak
your name and make you
think that no one could possibly
say it better than I can.

You are a mountain, and I promise,
I have the faith to move you.

The things
I want
never
wanted me back
until you.

I want to be the one
you think of on
long car rides
and sleepless nights.

The words
all sounded
so sweet

until I
found you
and realized

that words
are not
enough.

I love the way your lips feel on my neck,
and the way that I can always smell
vanilla on your breath.
Maybe it's because you're my favorite
and vanilla is my favorite too, so naturally
I can't separate the two— I don't know.
I'm just saying that I want you to
breathe me in whole like an inseparable part of
you.
I want to become you and have you become me
and create
something that could set the world on fire with
a single
careless movement. I want you and you want
me, but
a single mistaken flick of the wrist and everything
is in
flames.
We, two people who could
take over such a simple world on our own.
We, so high above them— untouchable from up
here.
We, together. Able to destroy as easily as we
create.
So dangerous. So scary. So beautiful.

You saw everything
that makes me a
good friend
and decided to
fall in love.

We both have a lot to learn.

I need to learn when all you're asking for is a tender moment. I need to know when to be soft despite my natural inclination to shrug things away.

And you, you need to learn to navigate my past while I do my best to be ready for our future.

We — we have so much to learn together.

I can't wait.

We write
poetry
together
that no one
else can see,
because some things
are just for
you & me.

Since I met you,
I've found
poetry
in back covers
of books
and in the pockets
of yesterday's clothes,

I find poetry
in the mixed colors
of your eyes
and in raindrops falling
from cloudy grey skies.

Since I met you,
I never know
where poetry
hides.

You are a moment I could live forever.

zack grey

I can't count the
I love you's anymore,
so let's number
the wrinkles on
each other's skin
until we can't
count those
either.

Sometimes you
say, "I hate you,"
and I smile at my
feet, thinking, 'yes,
I picked the
right one.'

You like to
leave me poetry
in the mornings
so I can wake up to
a piece of art,

forgetting
that I'm already
waking up
next to you.

The
meaning of
poetry
is
redefined
for me
every
day,

and today
poetry is
the way

you

sound
when you're
sleepy.

Show me where it hurts.
I'll place butterfly bandages
on every spot you point to,
not because they're most effective—
just because,
once in a while,
we all need to remember
that ugly things can
become beautiful

and learn to fly.

I just want to be the person you think I am.

To you,
I'm sweet nothings
& romance,

patience &
undiscovered dreams.

To you,
I'm a soft voice that could
charm a butterfly to sleep
& poetry in the
mornings.

I just want to be the person you think I am,
because

to me,
you're everything
that's right in this world.

When I meet you,
I'll breathe in deep,
let it all go,
and say, "finally."

About The Author:

He's smiling at you as you read this, watching the way your face changes with each new discovery, feeling like the
luckiest man in the world now that you've finally found him.

Acknowledgements:

I didn't work alone to make this for you. Thanks to everyone who helped me make our meeting so much more special. You know who you are.

Find Zack Grey on
Instagram, Facebook, and Tumblr @zackgreywrites.

CPSIA information can be obtained
at www.ICGtesting.com
Printed in the USA
BVOW08s2243011017
496432BV00016B/139/P